United States Government Accountability Office

Report to the Ranking Member, Committee on Foreign Relations, U.S. Senate

September 2013

CLIMATE CHANGE

State Should Further Improve Its Reporting on Financial Support to Developing Countries to Meet Future Requirements and Guidelines

GAO-13-829

CLIMATE CHANGE

State Should Further Improve Its Reporting on Financial Support to Developing Countries to Meet Future Requirements and Guidelines

Highlights of GAO-13-829, a report to the Ranking Member, Committee on Foreign Relations, United States Senate

Why GAO Did This Study

In 2009, the United States and other developed nations pledged to contribute funding approaching $30 billion in new and additional assistance between 2010 and 2012 for developing countries to address climate change. This type of assistance is called "climate finance" and funding for this period is known as "fast-start finance." The pledge was made under the Framework Convention, a treaty that seeks to address climate change. State is the lead agency responsible for reporting the United States' FSF contributions between 2010 and 2012 and plans to continue reporting on U.S. climate finance in the future. GAO was asked to review climate finance. This report examines (1) the extent to which the United States contributed to FSF, (2) how State collected and reported U.S. FSF data, and (3) what is known about the effectiveness of U.S. FSF activities. To address these objectives, GAO reviewed FSF data, interviewed agency officials, and visited three countries receiving significant FSF assistance in three regions.

What GAO Recommends

To ensure the United States meets future climate finance reporting requirements and guidelines under the Framework Convention, GAO recommends that State determine how it will collect and report climate finance information and review current capabilities for meeting the requirements and guidelines. GAO also recommends that State, in consultation with USAID, consider providing a budget code to improve tracking of climate change assistance. State agreed with GAO's recommendations.

View GAO-13-829. For more information, contact Thomas Melito at (202) 512-9601 or melitot@gao.gov, or J. Alfredo Gomez at (202) 512-4101 or gomezj@gao.gov.

What GAO Found

To implement the United States' fast-start finance (FSF) commitment, the Department of State (State) reported that the United States contributed $7.5 billion in fiscal years 2010 through 2012 for a variety of activities related to climate change. State, the U.S. Agency for International Development (USAID), and the Department of the Treasury (Treasury) provided $2.5 billion for activities under the Global Climate Change Initiative (GCCI) that were designed to address climate change as a primary goal. State reported that USAID and other agencies, including the Millennium Challenge Corporation (MCC), the Export-Import Bank of the United States, and the Overseas Private Investment Corporation provided $4.9 billion for activities that were not part of the GCCI but had climate-related benefits. Contributions consisted of grants, loans, development finance, and export credit. The majority of these funds were reported as supporting mitigation activities focused on clean energy or sustainable landscapes. According to State, the U.S. FSF contributions were "new and additional" because the funding was appropriated on an annual basis and not guaranteed from one year to the next.

Between 2010 and 2012, State improved its method for collecting data for its FSF reports, but it is uncertain how it will meet future reporting requirements and guidelines. Following its initial FSF report in fiscal year 2010, State developed a structured data collection tool to facilitate and standardize data collection across the agencies. Nonetheless, challenges in tracking climate change assistance remain. USAID, the largest FSF contributor, is not able to track climate change obligations and expenditures because of the lack of a dedicated State/USAID budget code for climate change assistance. While the FSF reports were voluntary, reporting is required beginning in 2014 based on decisions by the Conference of the Parties to the United Nations Framework Convention on Climate Change (Framework Convention). Future reports must contain climate finance data elements that State did not include in the FSF reports and, in some cases, does not currently collect. For example, State does not collect information on the annual status of climate finance contributions provided, committed, and/or pledged, as specified in the new reporting guidelines. State officials said that they have not determined how they will collect and report this information.

The overall effectiveness of U.S. FSF activities is difficult to determine because of the challenges involved in monitoring and evaluating assistance to address climate change. These challenges include difficulties in measuring the effects of individual activities within the larger context of global climate change, and the fact that many of these activities are just beginning to be implemented. Under the GCCI, State, USAID, and Treasury fund activities with a primary goal of addressing climate change, and State and USAID are refining their climate change performance indicators to improve monitoring of these activities' results. USAID is also drafting an evaluation plan for its climate change assistance. Treasury does not directly monitor and evaluate its climate change funding but requires the multilateral institutions that receive and implement this funding to monitor and evaluate these activities. Other key agencies' FSF activities were not part of the GCCI, and these agencies' approaches to monitoring and evaluation vary based on their respective missions and requirements. For example, MCC primarily assesses its projects on the basis of the progress made in achieving its goal of poverty reduction.

_____ United States Government Accountability Office

Contents

Figures

Abbreviations

CIF	Climate Investment Funds
EPA	Environmental Protection Agency
Ex-Im	Export-Import Bank of the United States
Framework Convention	United Nations Framework Convention on Climate Change
FSF	fast-start finance
GCCI	Global Climate Change Initiative
GEF	Global Environment Facility
MCC	Millennium Challenge Corporation
OMB	Office of Management and Budget
OPIC	Overseas Private Investment Corporation
State	Department of State
TFCA	Tropical Forest Conservation Act
Treasury	Department of the Treasury
USAID	U.S. Agency for International Development
USTDA	U.S. Trade and Development Agency

September 19, 2013

The Honorable Bob Corker
Ranking Member
Committee on Foreign Relations
United States Senate

Dear Senator Corker:

Increasing concentrations of greenhouse gases in the atmosphere have altered the earth's heat and radiation balance and contributed to changes in the earth's climate, according to the National Research Council and the United States Global Change Research Program. Greenhouse gases trap some of the sun's energy and prevent it from returning to space, warming the atmosphere. The effects of a warmer climate could have important consequences for human health and welfare by altering weather patterns, increasing the frequency and intensity of storms and droughts, changing crop yields, and contributing to flooding in coastal areas, among other things. While climate change can have positive and negative effects, the World Bank reported that the most pronounced negative effects are likely to occur in less economically developed countries.

In 2009, the United States and other developed countries jointly committed to providing developing countries with funding approaching $30 billion in assistance between 2010 and 2012 and committed to jointly mobilize $100 billion a year in public and private funds by 2020.[1] These funds are intended to be used for activities that aim to address the causes and impacts of climate change. We refer to this funding as "climate finance," and we refer to climate finance for the 2010 to 2012 period as "fast-start finance" (FSF). This commitment was made under the auspices of the United Nations Framework Convention on Climate Change (hereinafter referred to as the Framework Convention), a treaty that seeks to address the challenges posed by climate change, with 194 countries and the European Union as Parties.[2] The U.S. Department of State

---

[1]U.N. Doc. FCCC/CP/2009/11/Add.1, Dec. 2/CP.15, ¶ 8 (Dec. 18, 2009) [hereinafter Copenhagen Accord].

[2]See United Nations Framework Convention on Climate Change, U.N. Doc. A/AC237/18 (1992), reprinted in 31 I.L.M. 849 (1992) [hereinafter Framework Convention]; and Copenhagen Accord, ¶ 8.

(State) is the lead agency for international climate negotiations and for reporting to the secretariat of the Framework Convention on progress in fulfilling the U.S. climate finance commitments. In three annual reports to the Framework Convention secretariat, State reported on the amount and characteristics of U.S. FSF. Each report included a summary of the U.S. FSF funding, an overview of global and regional activities, and fact sheets on countries that received funding for that fiscal year.

You asked us to review aspects of the assistance the United States provided to address its FSF commitment under the Framework Convention. This report examines (1) the extent to which the United States contributed to FSF and the types of activities this funding supported, (2) how State collected and reported data on U.S. FSF funding and its plans for future reporting, and (3) what is known about the effectiveness of U.S. FSF activities.

To address these objectives, we focused primarily on the following six U.S. agencies that provided over 95 percent of the U.S. FSF funding: State, the U.S. Agency for International Development (USAID), the Department of the Treasury (Treasury), the Millennium Challenge Corporation (MCC), the Export-Import Bank of the United States (Ex-Im), and the Overseas Private Investment Corporation (OPIC). We interviewed agency officials and reviewed agency strategies, planning and programming documents, indicators, and monitoring and evaluation plans and reports. In addition, we reviewed and analyzed FSF funding data, criteria, and guidance. We also reviewed Framework Convention climate finance commitments, reporting guidelines, and requirements. We conducted fieldwork in three countries—Ethiopia, Indonesia, and Mexico—which we selected based on a range of factors, including FSF funding levels and sources, areas of focus, project implementation status, geographic diversity, country income level, recommendations from agencies, and congressional interest. These countries serve as illustrative and not representative examples. In these countries, we met with U.S. embassy officials and implementing partners, host-country government officials, multilateral development banks, and other bilateral donors. We also visited project sites and met with local implementing partners and recipients of the assistance. Appendix I provides more information on our scope and methodology.

We conducted this performance audit from May 2012 to September 2013 in accordance with generally accepted government auditing standards. Those standards require that we plan and perform the audit to obtain sufficient, appropriate evidence to provide a reasonable basis for our findings and conclusions based on our audit objectives. We believe that the evidence obtained provides a reasonable basis for our findings and conclusions based on our audit objectives.

Background

The Framework Convention Provides the Primary International Forum for Addressing Climate Change

In 1992, the United States and most other countries negotiated the Framework Convention with the aim of stabilizing atmospheric concentrations of carbon dioxide and five other greenhouse gases.[3] The Framework Convention includes a pledge from developed countries to assist developing countries in implementing these objectives.[4] The Framework Convention also recognizes the special situation of countries designated by the UN as least developed countries. The Conference of the Parties is the supreme decision-making body of the Framework Convention and all Parties to the Convention are represented at the Conference of the Parties. In 2001, the Conference of the Parties further noted that least developed countries have a lower capacity to cope with and adapt to the impacts of climate change, and recognized certain developing countries as particularly vulnerable to those impacts.

Efforts to address climate change under the Framework Convention generally fall into two categories—mitigation and adaptation. According to the Framework Convention, measures to mitigate climate change include efforts to limit manmade emissions of greenhouse gases and enhance greenhouse gas "sinks." The Framework Convention defines "sink" as any process, activity, or mechanism that removes a greenhouse gas, an aerosol, or a precursor of greenhouse gas from the atmosphere. For example, preserved forests, which store carbon dioxide, serve as greenhouse gas sinks. The burning of fossil fuels for energy accounts for about two-thirds of global manmade emissions. The remaining third stems from industrial and agricultural processes, land use changes such as deforestation, and waste such as methane emitted from landfills.

The Framework Convention website defines adaptation as adjustments in ecological, social, or economic systems in response to actual or expected

---

[3]The five other gases are methane, nitrous oxide, and three synthetic gases—hydrofluorocarbons, perfluorocarbons, and sulfur hexafluoride.

[4]Framework Convention, art. 4.

climate change and its effects, to alleviate potential damages or to benefit from opportunities associated with climate change.[5] For example, an adaptation effort might involve assessing vulnerabilities to rising sea levels, droughts, or fires, and then planning and executing activities that address these vulnerabilities.

Developed Countries Made Voluntary Climate Finance Commitments through the Framework Convention

One of the key outcomes of the 2009 meeting of the Conference of the Parties was the Copenhagen Accord. As part of the accord, the United States and other developed countries voluntarily pledged to provide up to $30 billion in "new and additional, predictable, and adequate" funding, now commonly known as fast-start finance, to help developing countries address climate change over the 2010 to 2012 period. According to State officials, the fast-start pledge, and the longer-term goal of mobilizing $100 billion per year from public and private sources by 2020, was critical to securing the broader 2009 Copenhagen Accord. State explained that the Copenhagen Accord included a commitment from major emerging economies to list, for the first time, the specific actions they would take to limit their emissions. Under this Accord, developed countries also agreed to a balanced allocation of resources between climate change mitigation and adaptation activities, with adaptation funding as a priority for countries most vulnerable to climate change impacts.[6] In addition, the Conference of the Parties established the Green Climate Fund, intended to centrally channel multilateral funding for climate finance. According to State and Treasury officials, as of July 2013, the design and structure of this institution was still under development, and the Fund was not yet operational.

In subsequent meetings of the Conference of the Parties, developed countries reaffirmed various Copenhagen climate finance commitments. At the Cancun meeting in 2010, the Conference of the Parties invited developed countries to submit information on their climate finance for the 2010 to 2012 FSF period to the secretariat of the Framework Convention for compilation into an information document. These reports during the FSF period were voluntary and were not based on specific reporting

---

[5]United Nations Framework Convention on Climate Change, "The Adaptation Process," *FOCUS: Adaptation*, accessed September 16, 2013, http://unfccc.int/focus/adaptation/items/6999.php.

[6]Under the Copenhagen Accord, priority countries for adaptation finance include least developed countries, small island developing states, and Africa. Copenhagen Accord ¶ 8.

requirements. At the 2011 meeting in Durban, the Conference of the Parties agreed to adopt reporting requirements and guidelines as part of required reports beginning in 2014. At the meeting in Durban, the Conference of the Parties also agreed that developed countries should

- describe how their financial assistance addresses the needs of developing countries regarding adaptation and mitigation;

- provide information on the financial assistance they provided, committed, and/or pledged to help developing parties mitigate greenhouse gas emissions or adapt to adverse effects of climate change and any economic and social consequences of response measures;

- describe the amount, type, funding source, financial instrument, and sector of their financial assistance, and indicate how they classified funding as new and additional; and

- report on their efforts to leverage private financial sources.

The Durban agreement also included provisions for developed countries to further develop plans for long-term climate finance beginning in 2012.

The United States Elevated Climate Change as a Development Priority

Following the FSF commitment, the United States elevated global climate change as a development priority through government-wide strategies. First, in May 2010, the White House issued the President's National Security Strategy, which emphasizes, among other things, the need to increase investments to address global climate change to improve the resilience of developing nations, minimize the impacts of climate change, conserve forests, and promote clean energy technologies. Then, in September 2010, the White House announced the Global Climate Change Initiative (GCCI), which seeks to integrate climate change considerations into foreign assistance.[7] According to State officials, the

---

[7]Following the GCCI announcement, the White House released in October 2010 a strategy document on reducing emissions from deforestation and forest degradation. This strategy outlines the U.S. approach for increasing carbon sequestration by forests in developing countries. In November 2010, State and USAID initiated the U.S. Government Enhancing Capacity for Low Emission Development Strategies program, an interagency effort to support developing countries' efforts to increase sustainable development while slowing the growth of emissions.

GAO-13-829 Climate Change

administration began placing a priority on assistance to address climate change in its fiscal year 2010 budget request, which reflected a significant increase over baseline funding levels. Beginning in fiscal year 2010, State, USAID, and Treasury began receiving annual appropriations that were used to finance a wide range of bilateral and multilateral programs and activities under the GCCI. The GCCI focuses U.S. efforts to address global climate change within three pillars, or areas of focus—adaptation, clean energy, and sustainable landscapes. Specifically, State describes activities within each of these pillars as follows:

- *Adaptation activities* increase resilience to climate change for the most vulnerable communities in areas such as food security, water management, coastal management, and public health by helping communities respond to increasing climate and weather-related risks.

- *Clean energy activities* support decreasing emissions growth through mitigation activities such as the deployment of clean energy technologies, policies, and practices. They often include support for infrastructure projects. According to State, the United States' clean energy activities focus on countries and sectors offering significant emission growth reduction potential over the long term, as well as countries that offer the potential to demonstrate leadership in sustained, large-scale deployment of clean energy.

- *Sustainable landscapes activities* focus largely on helping countries address unsustainable forest clearing and support the sustainable management of forests at the national and local levels. The United States' sustainable landscape efforts focus on developing countries such as Indonesia and Mexico that have demonstrated a commitment to address climate change and have a high potential to reduce emissions from deforestation, forest degradation, and other land-use activities.

The Framework Convention and the GCCI have similar areas of focus, although two of the U.S. GCCI pillars—sustainable landscapes and clean energy activities—involve activities defined as mitigation activities under the Framework Convention (see fig. 1).

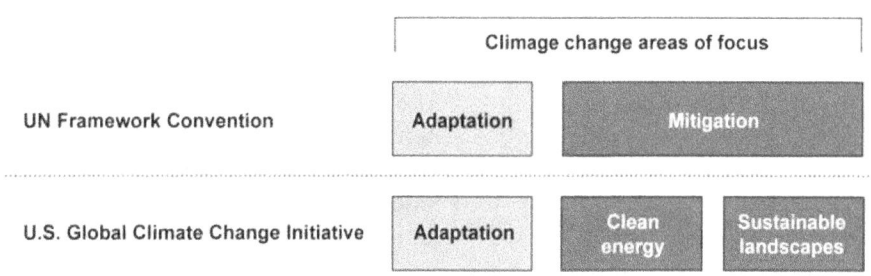

Figure 1: Comparison of Areas of Focus within UN Framework Convention and U.S. Global Climate Change Initiative Pillars

Source: GAO analysis of State and UN data

State Reported That the United States Contributed $7.5 Billion to FSF, Supporting a Variety of Activities

To implement its FSF commitment, State reported that, from fiscal year 2010 through 2012, the United States contributed $7.5 billion to support a variety of activities that address the causes and impacts of climate change. U.S. FSF funding included activities that were part of the GCCI and were designed to address climate change as a primary goal, as well as activities that were not part of the GCCI, but were reported to have climate-related benefits. U.S. FSF funding included a variety of financial instruments, such as grants, loans, loan guarantees,[8] and export credit insurance.[9] The majority of the U.S. FSF funds supported mitigation activities focused on clean energy or sustainable landscapes. According to State officials, all U.S. FSF funding was considered to be "new and additional" resources because the funding was appropriated on an annual basis. State, USAID, and Treasury financed activities with a primary goal of addressing climate change, as part of the GCCI, which represented about one-third of total U.S. FSF funding.[10] USAID and agencies such as MCC, Ex-Im, and OPIC, provided funding for activities that they reported as having climate-related benefits but were not funded as part of the GCCI. This funding represented about two-thirds of total U.S. FSF

---

[8]Loan guarantees cover the repayment risks on the foreign borrower's debt obligations, guaranteeing a lender that, in the event of a payment default by the borrower, the agency will pay the outstanding principal and interest.

[9]Export credit insurance helps U.S. exporters sell their goods overseas by protecting them against the risk of foreign buyer or other foreign debtor default for political or commercial reasons, allowing them to extend credit to their international customers for short-term or medium-term sales.

[10]According to State, 98.7 percent of federal funds that supported activities as part of the GCCI activities counted toward the U.S. FSF commitment

funding. These non-GCCI activities may have primary goals other than addressing climate change, such as poverty reduction and food security, but they were reported to have climate-related benefits.

State Reported That Multiple U.S. Agencies Contributed $7.5 Billion over the FSF Period, Largely for Mitigation Activities

State reported that 17 U.S. agencies contributed a total of $7.5 billion to FSF in fiscal years 2010 to 2012, largely for activities with mitigation benefits.[11] Six of the 17 agencies—State, USAID, Treasury, MCC, Ex-Im, and OPIC—provided about 97 percent of the total $7.5 billion in U.S. FSF funding, according to State documents. Figure 2 shows the breakdown of total U.S. FSF funding by key agency.

[11]The 17 agencies were State; USAID; Treasury; MCC; Ex-Im; OPIC; the Departments of Commerce, Defense, and Energy; the Environmental Protection Agency (EPA); National Aeronautics and Space Administration; National Oceanic and Atmospheric Administration; National Science Foundation; U.S. Army Corps of Engineers; U.S. Forest Service; U.S. Trade and Development Agency; and the Peace Corps.

Figure 2: Total U.S. Fast-Start Finance (FSF) Funding by Agency, Fiscal Years 2010-2012 (dollars in millions)

Total $7,457 (Dollars in millions)

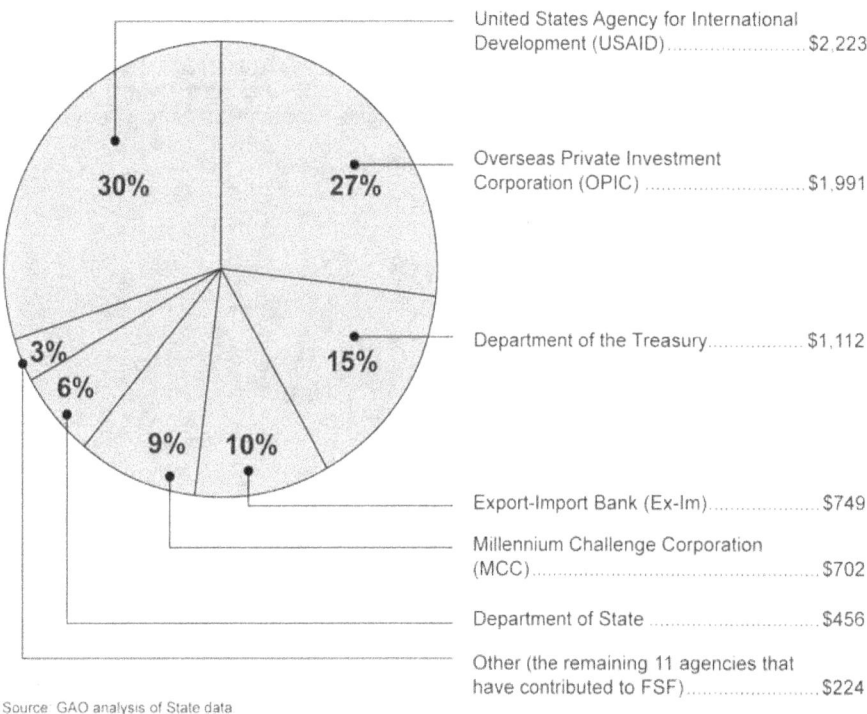

United States Agency for International Development (USAID)......................$2,223

Overseas Private Investment Corporation (OPIC) $1,991

Department of the Treasury.................$1,112

Export-Import Bank (Ex-Im)....................$749

Millennium Challenge Corporation (MCC)...$702

Department of State $456

Other (the remaining 11 agencies that have contributed to FSF).......................$224

Source: GAO analysis of State data

About 80 percent ($6.1 billion) of the total U.S. FSF funding supported mitigation activities and the remaining 20 percent ($1.4 billion) supported adaptation activities. While developed countries agreed to provide a "balanced allocation for adaptation and mitigation," the Copenhagen Accord did not define the meaning of a "balanced allocation."[12] State officials told us that in the absence of such a definition, State's approach to the U.S. FSF commitment was to focus on those activities that were most cost effective and had the greatest near-term impact, and that these tended to be mitigation activities. State officials also said that the United States planned to develop and expand adaptation activities in the future.

---

[12]During the FSF period, Australia reported contributing its FSF funds roughly equally between adaptation and mitigation activities. Many other countries reported contributing more toward mitigation than adaptation activities.

GAO-13-829 Climate Change

Figure 3 shows U.S. FSF funding for adaptation and mitigation activities in each of the three FSF years, as reported by State. According to State's FSF report, U.S. funding for mitigation activities was provided in the form of grants, loans, loan guarantees, or insurance assistance, whereas U.S. funding for adaptation activities was provided solely in the form of grants.

Figure 3: U.S. Fast-Start Finance (FSF) Funding by Adaptation and Mitigation Activities, Fiscal Years 2010 through 2012 (dollars in millions)

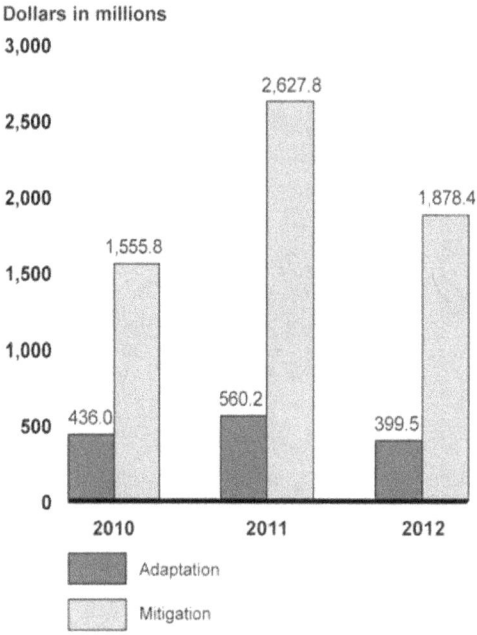

Source: GAO analysis of State's 2012 FSF Report.

Note: State's 2012 FSF report includes climate finance data from fiscal years 2010-2012.

While developed countries pledged to provide "new and additional resources," the Copenhagen Accord did not define this term or specify the level of funding that each nation would provide to reach the overall target. State officials said that the United States defined "new and additional resources" as any funding appropriated for activities addressing climate change in a given year because appropriations are enacted each year and therefore are not guaranteed in future years. Hence, under State's definition, all funding allocated from an appropriation in a given year is considered "new and additional" even if the activities had been funded in prior years. For example, as part of U.S. FSF funding, State included a total of $107.8 million from State and the Environmental Protection Agency (EPA) for the Multilateral Fund for the Implementation of the

Montreal Protocol, which was established in 1990. According to UN officials, the definition of "new and additional" varies by country and only a few countries have publicly stated their definition. For example, Germany defined "new and additional" as funds that were "additional to the support related to addressing climate change already provided in 2009, as well as sourced from innovative financing mechanisms, namely the auctioning of emissions certificates."[13]

State officials said that the United States increased its funding to address climate change after the FSF commitment. Before the commitment, State collected data from State, USAID, and Treasury on activities with a primary goal of addressing the causes and impacts of climate change, and State reported that funding for these activities tripled from 2009 to 2010. During the 2010 to 2012 FSF period, State continued to collect data on such activities and categorized them as part of the GCCI. State also began to collect data on other activities from USAID and from additional agencies, including Ex-Im and OPIC, which were reported as having climate-related benefits but were not funded as part of the GCCI. For this report, we define the latter type of activity as "non-GCCI activities." These activities may not have a primary goal of addressing climate change. For example, the development and distribution of drought-resistant seeds as part of a USAID food security project is intended to decrease the vulnerability of farmers in food-insecure areas. It also can be considered as a non-GCCI climate adaptation activity because it helps communities respond to increasing climate risks.

GCCI Activities, with a Primary Goal of Addressing Climate Change, Represented One-Third of Total U.S. FSF Funding

GCCI activities implemented by State, USAID, and Treasury with a primary goal of addressing global climate change represented about one-third of U.S. FSF funding. State reported that these three agencies provided about $2.5 billion for these activities from appropriations enacted for foreign operations over the FSF period. These agencies are the core implementers of the GCCI and addressing global climate change is a part of each of these agencies' overall strategies. Table 1 shows the agencies' funding for GCCI activities with a primary goal of addressing climate change, funding for non-GCCI activities, and total contributions to U.S. FSF funding.

---

[13]Generally, emissions certificates are tradable permits in a cap-and-trade program, in which an overall emissions cap is set. Entities covered by the program must hold these certificates to cover their emissions.

Table 1: Funding for Global Climate Change Initiative (GCCI) Activities, Non-GCCI Activities, and Total U.S. Fast-Start Finance (FSF) Funding by Agency, Fiscal Years 2010-2012 (dollars in millions)

Agency	Funding for GCCI activities	Funding for non-GCCI activities	Total FSF funding
State	$455	$1	**$456**
USAID[a]	$1,022	$1,201	**$2,223**
Treasury	$1,112	$0	**$1,112**
MCC[b]	$0	$702	**$702**
Ex-Im[c]	$0	$749	**$749**
OPIC[d]	$0	$1,991	**$1,991**
Other[e]	$0	$224	**$224**
Total	**2,589**	**4,868**	**7,457**

Source: GAO analysis of State data.

Notes:

[a]U.S. Agency for International Development (USAID).

[b]Millennium Challenge Corporation (MCC).

[c]Export-Import Bank (Ex-Im).

[d]Overseas Private Investment Corporation (OPIC).

[e]"Other" represents the remaining 11 agencies that have contributed to FSF.

State and USAID Contributed U.S. FSF Funding through Bilateral and Multilateral Assistance

Over the 2010 to 2012 FSF period, State contributed $455 million in funds to developing countries to support activities with a primary goal of addressing global climate change as part of the GCCI. State finances bilateral and multilateral activities in partnership with other U.S. agencies and multilateral funds. For example, State provided bilateral funding for the U.S. Africa Clean Energy Finance initiative with a goal of mobilizing U.S. investments in clean energy and energy efficiency across Africa.

State also contributed toward the Least Developed Countries Fund, a multilateral fund supporting urgent adaptation needs of least developed countries. In Ethiopia, for example, the Least Developed Countries Fund helped design and implement adaptation activities, such as planting fruit trees to provide additional food sources and to reforest the land, to reduce vulnerability to the effects of climate change.

Source: GAO.

Over the FSF period, USAID contributed over $1 billion in the form of grants to developing countries for GCCI activities that counted toward U.S. FSF. For example, USAID's activities that address climate change in Mexico include mitigation projects supporting the development of the country's low emissions development strategy, the planning and development of a strategy to reduce emissions from deforestation and degradation, and the development of systems to monitor progress against the strategies' goals. For instance, USAID is working with the U.S. Forest Service to improve Mexico's capacity for monitoring, reporting, and verification of carbon stored in forests (see sidebar). Starting in fiscal year 2010, USAID reported increased funding for activities designed to promote adaptation and increased funding for mitigation activities to a lesser extent. Toward the end of the FSF period, USAID released its 5-year Climate Change and Development Strategy, intended to strengthen the integration of climate change into USAID programming and accelerate the implementation of activities that focus on adaptation and low emissions development.[14]

---

[14]State and USAID officials commented that with the inclusion of an integration objective, the Strategy made it USAID policy to incorporate climate change risks and mitigation opportunities into the broader portfolio of USAID programming, in particular into USAID missions' Country Development and Coordination strategies.

Treasury FSF Contributions Largely Supported Multilateral Clean Energy Activities

State reported that Treasury contributed about $1.1 billion toward U.S. FSF funding mostly through contributions to multilateral funds that finance activities promoting adaptation, clean energy, and sustainable landscapes.[15] According to Treasury officials, these multilateral funds provide concessional loans and grants through multilateral development banks and other international institutions. After the FSF commitment and in line with the GCCI, Treasury acknowledged the importance of addressing climate change in its strategic plan. Over the FSF period, the majority of Treasury funding—about $915 million—supported the multilateral Climate Investment Funds (CIF), which involve financing instruments to support developing countries' efforts to mitigate and manage the challenges of climate change by providing grants and other financing instruments that leverage financing from the private sector, multilateral development banks, and other sources.[16] For example, one investment fund—the Clean Technology Fund—provided a loan for a private-sector clean energy wind farm in Mexico. Another financing instrument—the Forest Investment Program—will be used to provide loans and grants to the government of Indonesia to develop activities to reduce deforestation and forest degradation and promote forest management.

State reported that Treasury also contributed about $196 million to two other programs, the Global Environment Facility (GEF) and the Tropical Forest Conservation Act's bilateral debt-for-nature program. According to Treasury, the GEF is intended to help developing countries address biodiversity, climate change, and other environmental problems.[17] In East Africa, for example, the GEF supported sustainable transportation

---

[15]State officials noted that neither the United States nor any other country considers contributions to the general resources of the World Bank or other multilateral development banks as part of the FSF contribution.

[16]The CIF consist of the Clean Technology Fund and the Strategic Climate Fund, which are implemented through the multilateral development banks. The Clean Technology Fund seeks to provide developing and middle income countries with incentives to scale up technologies with a high potential for long-term greenhouse gas emissions savings. The Strategic Climate Fund supports programs to promote sustainable forest management, integrate climate resilience into development, and scale up renewable energy solutions in the world's poorest countries.

[17]The GEF, established in October 1991 to promote global environmental protection and environmentally sustainable development, is an institution that serves as a financial mechanism for the Framework Convention and several other international conventions. Since 1994, the World Bank has served as the Trustee of the GEF Trust Fund and provided administrative services.

solutions. State included about 50 percent (about $148 million) of Treasury's contribution to the GEF as part of FSF. Treasury officials stated that 26 percent of the trust fund's projects support clean energy and 24 percent focus on sustainable land use, while the remaining 50 percent do not focus on addressing climate change and are not included as FSF. State also included as FSF funding all of Treasury's contributions, about $48 million, to the Tropical Forest Conservation Act's bilateral debt-for-nature program. Under this program, the United States "redirects" debt payments that would have been due to the U.S. government into forest conservation funds in the beneficiary country. These funds make grants, mainly to local nongovernmental organizations and community groups, to support forest conservation activities.[18]

Non-GCCI Activities Represented about Two-Thirds of U.S. FSF Funding

Over the 2010 to 2012 FSF period, non-GCCI activities with reported climate-related benefits, implemented by multiple agencies, represented about two-thirds of U.S. FSF funding. According to U.S. agency officials, these activities were counted toward the U.S. FSF commitment but were not necessarily funded as a result of the commitment. State reported that 16 agencies provided about $4.9 billion that was counted toward FSF through these non-GCCI activities. Four agencies—USAID, MCC, Ex-Im, and OPIC—provided the majority of this funding, representing almost $4.6 billion of the reported U.S. FSF total contributions (see table 1 above).[19] These four agencies used different mechanisms to finance non-GCCI activities, with USAID and MCC providing grants, Ex-Im providing export credit,[20] and OPIC providing development finance.[21] Over the FSF period, total U.S. funding for non-GCCI activities varied from about $1.1 billion in fiscal year 2010 to $2.4 billion in 2011, to $1.4 billion in fiscal year 2012.

---

[18]These local programs are governed by boards that include representatives from local environmental groups and institutions, the U.S. government, and the beneficiary government.

[19]The other 12 agencies provided a total of $225 million that was counted toward the FSF contribution for activities that have climate-related benefits.

[20]Ex-Im serves as the official export credit agency of the United States and helps U.S. firms export goods and services by providing a range of financial products, including direct loans, loan guarantees, and insurance.

[21]OPIC provides development finance through financing, loan guarantees, political risk insurance, and support for private equity investment funds.

USAID and MCC Provided Grants to Fund Non-GCCI Activities with Climate-Related Benefits

USAID provided $1.2 billion in grants for activities that primarily supported development needs such as food security and global health but were also reported to have climate-related benefits. These non-GCCI activities also may be counted toward other government goals and initiatives. For example, USAID supports climate change adaptation activities in Ethiopia, which USAID implemented as part of its food security program. As part of the President's Feed the Future initiative, the USAID mission in Ethiopia initiated a multiyear food security project that promotes increasing agricultural growth capacity in several chronically food-insecure areas of the country and also incorporates adaptation activities such as introducing drought-resistant crops. According to State and USAID in Ethiopia, these activities also have reported climate-related benefits because they reduce vulnerability to climate change. The USAID Ethiopia mission also supported other activities that had reported climate change adaptation benefits—such as land rehabilitation and construction of irrigation structures—as part of its contribution to the Productive Safety Net Program that the government of Ethiopia launched in 2005 to address chronic food insecurity (see sidebar).

In the FSF reports, State included $702 million in grants from MCC for non-GCCI activities because parts of MCC's compact grants are reported to support activities with climate-related benefits in five developing countries. Four of the five compacts were signed during the FSF period, and one was signed prior to the commitment.[22][23] For example, MCC signed a compact with the government of Indonesia for a total of $588 million of which $332 million supported a project (known as the Green Prosperity Project) intended to increase renewable energy and sustainable land use practices, and strengthen the capacity for low carbon development. In another example, MCC signed a compact with the government of Moldova in which, in conjunction with its investment in

USAID Dam Project in Ethiopia Supported Adaptation to Climate Change

As part of USAID's efforts to improve food security to rural communities in Ethiopia that experience increasingly frequent droughts, USAID funds dam construction to help collect silt and store rainwater. The dam below was built in partnership with USAID. According to project implementers, the dam collects rainwater as it flows down the valley, which reduces erosion and replenishes moisture in the soil while retaining rainwater for future use.

Source: GAO.

---

[22]State officials explained that they counted the Mongolia Compact as part of the U.S. FSF contribution even though it was signed in 2008, because it was amended during the FSF period. The compact's amendment added a new project specifically relating to reducing urban air pollution by aiding the adoption of more energy efficient technologies.

[23]MCC officials commented that MCC generally reported all relevant FSF funding for compacts based on the year the compact was signed. However, only a small portion of the compact amount is obligated at signing, and the balance of the MCC funding is obligated at entry into force.

the rehabilitation of several large irrigation systems, MCC is funding a $2 million river basin management program to improve Moldova's capacity to manage its limited water resources in light of increasing demand for water and the expected effect of climate change. MCC's goal is to reduce poverty by addressing the partner countries' priorities for achieving sustainable economic growth, which may involve addressing climate change impacts. According to MCC officials, the agency has no specific goals or objectives related to climate change, but its agreements can link poverty reduction and development with climate-related goals when a country's priorities involve climate change concerns.

Ex-Im Provided Export Finance and OPIC Provided Development Finance for Non-GCCI Activities

Ex-Im Financed a Wind Farm in Mexico That Supported Clean Energy as a Climate-Related Benefit

Ex-Im provided a loan for exporting U.S. manufactured wind turbines to a wind farm in Oaxaca, Mexico, pictured below. This wind farm harnesses wind energy and connects to Mexico's national grid. It is the same wind farm that also received a loan from the Clean Technology Fund, to which Treasury provided funds.

Source: GAO.

According to State's 2012 FSF report, Ex-Im provided about $750 million through a range of financial products—such as direct loans, loan guarantees, and insurance—that supported non-GCCI clean energy activities. For Ex-Im's financial products, State counted the nominal value of Ex-Im's commitments made to eligible projects during the 2010 to 2012 FSF period. For example, Ex-Im provided nearly $200,000 in insurance to a solar power-generating system in Mexico; State included this entire liability amount toward the FSF total. According to Ex-Im officials, Ex-Im's export finance that supports clean energy projects is part of its larger mission to help U.S. firms export goods. Ex-Im has a carbon policy that aims to increase the private sector incentives and demand for renewable energy exports. This followed a congressional directive that at least 10 percent of Ex-Im's annual authorizations should be used for renewable energy technologies or energy efficient end-use technologies.[24] According to Ex-Im officials, the agency has struggled to meet this target because of the market-driven nature of its work and because it can only fund activities with a reasonable expectation of repayment. On the basis of our prior work, we found that Ex-Im faces challenges in achieving its target but has increased its clean energy financing since the FSF commitment.[25] (See the sidebar for an example of an Ex-Im financed clean energy project.)

State reported that during the 2010 to 2012 FSF period, OPIC provided about $2 billion for development finance that supported non-GCCI activities through a range of financial products such as loans, loan

---

[24]See Omnibus Appropriations Act, 2009, Pub. L. No. 111-8, 123 Stat. 524, 858.

[25]GAO, *Export-Import Bank: Additional Analysis and Information Could Better Inform Congress on Exposure, Risk, and Resources*, GAO-13-620 (Washington, D.C.: May 30, 2013).

GAO-13-829 Climate Change

guaranties, and insurance. In general, OPIC provides development finance for clean energy projects as part of its larger mission to support U.S. private investment in emerging markets. As with Ex-Im, State counted the nominal value of OPIC's commitments to eligible projects during the fast-start period. For example, OPIC provided an investment guarantee of $20.3 million for the construction of two hydroelectric facilities in Mexico; State included the value of that loan toward the U.S. FSF funding total. OPIC also has an Environmental and Social Policy Statement that responds to a congressional requirement to reduce direct greenhouse gas emissions associated with projects in OPIC's portfolio by 30 percent over 10 years.[26] According to State, OPIC financing with climate-related benefits has increased substantially, from about $8.9 million in 2008 to an average of $663.8 million annually during the FSF period.

State Improved Its Data Collection over the FSF Reporting Period, but Has Not Determined How It Will Meet Future Reporting Requirements and Guidelines

State improved its method for collecting data for its FSF reports, but it is uncertain how it will meet future reporting requirements and guidelines agreed to under the Framework Convention. After the FSF commitment, State faced a new and difficult challenge in collecting and reporting on U.S. assistance to developing countries to address climate change. Following its initial FSF report in fiscal year 2010, State developed a structured data collection tool to facilitate and standardize data collection across the agencies. Even with the data collection tool, challenges for tracking assistance remain. State and USAID do not have a dedicated budget code for tracking climate change assistance. With USAID climate change funding allocated to numerous missions, USAID, the largest FSF contributor, is unable to track GCCI obligations and expenditures and must undertake a manual inventory to obtain information on the types of climate change programs its missions are undertaking. While the current FSF report submissions are voluntary, reporting is required beginning in 2014 based on decisions adopted by the Conference of the Parties.[27] Future reports must contain certain data elements on each country's climate finance contributions that State did not include in the FSF reports and, in some cases, does not currently collect. State officials stated that they have not determined how they will collect and report this information.

[26]22 U.S.C. § 2191b.

[27]See U.N. Doc. FCCC/CP/2011/9/Add.1, decision 2/CP.17, ¶¶ 12-5 (Dec. 11, 2011).

State Improved Its Data Collection Process for the 2011 and 2012 Reports

Following the December 2009 FSF commitment, State faced challenges collecting data on agencies' FSF contributions but improved its data collection process during the 2010 to 2012 FSF period. Specifically, State faced challenges collecting data on fiscal year 2010 contributions from agencies for the initial FSF report but in fiscal year 2011 established a data collection tool in collaboration with the Office of Management and Budget (OMB) and developed a database for tracking FSF information. According to State officials, State's method for collecting and reporting FSF data in fiscal year 2010 was less structured than in the following 2 years because the United States decided to prepare the FSF report partway through that fiscal year and State did not have time to develop a structured data collection tool.

For fiscal year 2010, State gathered information on its own FSF activities and those of USAID as part of State and USAID's broader annual process to develop internal operational plans.[28] State and USAID's guidance on compiling these operational plans included definitions of activities with addressing climate change as a primary goal and activities with climate-related benefits, along with a list of eligible FSF activities under each of the three GCCI pillars. State did not, however, have an existing process to collect these data from other agencies that contributed to FSF. State officials said they reached out to individual agencies to obtain information on funding level, administering agency, and intended climate change benefits of each FSF activity. However, these officials stated that they faced challenges in obtaining FSF data from agencies other than State and USAID for the 2010 report.

For fiscal years 2011 and 2012, State established a structured data collection tool and developed guidance in collaboration with OMB to facilitate and standardize data collection for the 15 agencies other than State and USAID. This guidance included criteria that agencies could use to determine if an activity should count toward FSF. For those years, State collected data on its own FSF activities and those of USAID through the process to develop internal operational plans, as it had for the 2010 report, and asked OMB for assistance in collecting FSF data from the remaining agencies.[29] State then worked with OMB to develop the data

---

[28]The operational plans contained 1-year implementation plans and budget information for each country's State and USAID mission office and included data on climate change funding and activities, which State used for the FSF reports.

[29]OMB did not assist State in collecting FSF data for fiscal year 2010 but did review the budget information that State collected, according to officials from both agencies.

collection tool for collecting FSF data from those agencies. According to State officials, OMB's participation in the data collection effort improved the FSF data obtained from other agencies for the 2011 and 2012 reports. The tool consisted of a template for requesting data such as the name of the relevant activity, funding level, recipient country, and narrative description. State and OMB developed guidance to accompany the tool, which officials from both agencies said included a modified version of the guidance used by State and USAID to develop their operational plans and an adapted list of eligible FSF activities.[30]

State did not create a database to compile the FSF submissions for the 2010 report but developed one for the 2011 and 2012 reports. In fiscal year 2010, State compiled the FSF data in a narrative document that became the 2010 FSF report. By fiscal year 2011, State had developed a database for FSF submissions that included aggregated funding data at the country, pillar, and agency level but did not include funding data at the individual activity level. In fiscal year 2012, State improved the database by tracking the funding data at the individual activity level.

State officials said that for each of the 3 years, they went through an extensive review process to determine whether data included in the agencies' submissions should count toward the reported FSF total. These officials stated that a small group of State staff reviewed and discussed the submissions, using their judgment to determine if they should qualify for FSF. In some cases, the review process involved follow-up discussions with agency officials. State officials said that the review process for each of the three FSF reports took approximately 3 months.

State and USAID Do Not Have a Dedicated Budget Code for Tracking Assistance to Address Climate Change

While State has improved its process for collecting FSF data with these changes, some challenges remain in tracking USAID's climate finance data. According to USAID officials, State and USAID currently do not have a dedicated budget code for assistance that addresses climate change, which has created difficulties for tracking and gathering USAID data on such funding. USAID's budget and accounting systems link to State and USAID's standardized program structure for foreign assistance,

---

[30]State and OMB officials said that they adapted the list of eligible FSF activities so that the activities on the revised list would align more closely with those implemented by agencies other than State and USAID.

which is sometimes referred to as the foreign assistance framework.[31] This structure establishes a hierarchy of strategic objectives, program areas, program elements, and sub-elements. USAID officials stated that USAID's financial managers currently code obligations down to the program element level but not the sub-element level. Therefore, USAID does not have obligation data for assistance that addresses climate change because climate change is currently a sub-element. Specifically, climate change is one of eight sub-elements under the Clean Productive Environment program element (see table 2).

Table 2: Placement of Climate Change as a Sub-Element in State and USAID's Foreign Assistance Framework

Strategic Objective 4: Economic Growth
Program Area 4.8: Environment
Program Element 4.8.1 Natural Resources and Biodiversity
Program Element 4.8.2 Clean Productive Environment
Sub-Element 4.8.2.1 Clean Productive Environment Policy and Guidance
Sub-Element 4.8.2.2 Clean Production
Sub-Element 4.8.2.3 Clean Energy
Sub-Element 4.8.2.4 Climate Change
Sub-Element 4.8.2.5 Air Quality
Sub-Element 4.8.2.6 Sound Management of Waste
Sub-Element 4.8.2.7 Toxic Substances
Sub-Element 4.8.2.8 Science and Technology as a Tool for Environmental Decision-Making

Source: State.

The absence of a dedicated budget code has implications for tracking climate change assistance. According to USAID officials, to track climate change programs below the level of which GCCI pillar they are in (adaptation, clean energy, or sustainable landscapes), USAID has to manually gather climate change funding data through a time-consuming

---

[31]The standardized program structure was jointly developed by State and USAID to establish a consistent way to categorize and account for foreign assistance managed by State and USAID. This structure includes five strategic objectives of U.S. foreign assistance—Peace and Security, Governing Justly and Democratically, Investing in People, Economic Growth, and Humanitarian Assistance—and defines the full set of program areas and associated activities that fall under these strategic objectives and establishes standard indicators for measuring performance.

inventory of the numerous USAID missions' climate change programs. USAID's accounting database tracks the program element code 4.8.2 (Clean Productive Environment), but this code also encompasses funding other than climate change funding. In addition, not all climate change funding may appear under the Climate Change sub-element 4.8.2.4. Funds that support activities that address climate change may also appear under other program element codes, such as natural resources and biodiversity. These officials stated that elevating climate change to a higher-level program area within the standardized program structure would provide several benefits, including enabling them to better track the agency's activities that address climate change and related funding. This could also enhance the efficiency of efforts to track U.S. assistance that addresses climate change, which is a long-term priority of the administration and an integral component of U.S. commitments made through the Framework Convention.

The foreign assistance standardized program structure also serves as the foundation for State and USAID's budget requests, annual operational plans, and performance reporting. The continuing categorization of climate change as a sub-element rather than as a program area does not appear to reflect State and USAID's actions emphasizing climate change as a high priority. For example, State and USAID have included climate change as one of eight outcome-focused agency priority goals that reflect the highest priorities of both the Secretary of State and the USAID Administrator. According to State and USAID, these near-term goals advance the agencies' joint strategic goals and reflect their strategic and budget priorities.

State and USAID officials said that State's Foreign Assistance Bureau is leading a broader review of the foreign assistance standardized program structure, but State officials did not provide us with a time frame for completing this review. These officials stated that any changes to the standardized program structure would have implications for consistency with prior years. In addition, changing the placement of climate change within the structure would also affect the categorization of other environmental programs, and these considerations must be thought through carefully before making any changes.

The FSF Reports Contained Country Fact Sheets with Activity Descriptions, but Did Not Include All FSF Activities and Funding

State voluntarily issued three annual FSF reports that included summary discussions of the U.S. funding totals and more detailed country fact sheets with descriptions of activities; however, the reports did not include a full list of all FSF activities and their funding levels or information on the disbursement status of FSF activities. State officials said that the FSF reports were intended for the diplomatic objective of demonstrating U.S. progress in meeting its fast-start commitment. State officials said that they shared the country fact sheets with some developing countries at conferences and negotiations and that this met their diplomatic objective of demonstrating to developing countries that the United States was providing adequate climate finance and meeting its commitment.

Regarding the reports' content, each report included fact sheets on some of the countries that received funding for that fiscal year. However, the fact sheets, as noted in the 2012 FSF report, did not capture information on some sensitive activities. The country fact sheets provided high-level information on total bilateral and multilateral development finance and export credit contributions, and narrative descriptions of some FSF activities that included the funding level, administering agency, target beneficiaries, and intended climate change benefits of each reported activity. For example, the 2011 Mexico fact sheet noted that USAID provided $7 million to support the Government of Mexico in completing and implementing its national strategy to reduce greenhouse gas emissions from deforestation, focusing on helping the country strengthen relevant policy frameworks and build institutional and technical capacity that would reduce the rate of deforestation. While the fact sheet provided funding information on the aggregate level and provided examples of some individual activities, it did not identify all of the activities supported by the $7 million under Mexico's national strategy.

According to State officials, the FSF reports were not intended as a financial accounting exercise. Because the FSF reports do not provide a full list of all the activities and their funding levels, it was not possible for us or other external parties to verify the reported $7.5 billion contribution over the FSF period. For fiscal years 2010 and 2011, two nongovernmental organizations tried to recreate the reported total and were unable to account for the total reported amount.[32] One was able to

---

[32]The two nongovernmental organizations were the World Resources Institute, a policy research organization focused on environmental and socioeconomic development issues, and Climate Advisors, a consulting firm focused on U.S. climate change policy and international climate cooperation.

account for 91 percent of the total by analyzing publicly available information, and the other said that it was difficult to reconcile the numbers from the FSF reports with other publicly available budget data.

In addition, the FSF reports also did not include information on the disbursement status of FSF activities because State did not request disbursement information from other agencies and, instead, it requested that agencies report on the amounts either appropriated or obligated, which it included in the FSF reports using broad characterizations such as "amount provided" or "investments." At any given time, the amount disbursed can vary from the amount appropriated or obligated, and the amount in the FSF reports may not have reflected the implementation status of the activity.

During our country site visits, we found examples of projects that were included in the FSF reports but had not begun implementation. State included a $332 million MCC project in Indonesia in the 2011 FSF report, but we found that the agreement for that project did not enter into force until April 2013 and that MCC had not disbursed project funding as of June 2013. In another example, State reported a $50 million OPIC activity in the 2011 Indonesia fact sheet but the activity had not begun implementation at the time of our January 2013 site visit to Indonesia, and an OPIC official said the "future success [of the project] appeared to be highly improbable." OPIC reported that its $50 million commitment to the investment fund was canceled on May 14, 2013.

Future Climate Finance Reporting Will Require Information That Was Not Included in the FSF Reports, and State Has Not Determined How it Will Address These Requirements and Guidelines

Climate finance reporting requirements and guidelines under the Framework Convention have evolved, and State plans to continue reporting on U.S. climate finance contributions; however, State has yet to determine how it will collect and report on this information in the future. In contrast to the current voluntary nature of the FSF report submissions to the secretariat of the Framework Convention, reporting will be required beginning in 2014 based on decisions adopted by the Conference of the Parties in Durban in 2011 and in Doha in 2012.[33] The Conference of the Parties decided that developed countries shall submit their first biennial reports to the Framework Convention secretariat in January 2014 and use specific reporting guidelines for the biennial reports to ensure that

---

[33]U.N. Doc. FCCC/CP/2011/9/Add.1, decision 2/CP.17 (Dec. 11, 2011) and UN Doc. FCCC/CP/2012/8/Add.3, decision 19/CP.18 (Dec. 8, 2012).

countries provided consistent, transparent, comparable, accurate, and complete information (see table 3 for a comparison of future reporting criteria relative to the information currently collected and provided in the FSF reports).[34] The Conference of the Parties also plans to consider the best approach for future reporting on climate-related private finance at the next meeting when it discusses the reporting guidelines.

Table 3: Comparison of the Future Framework Convention Biennial Reporting Criteria and State's Current Data Collection for Climate Finance

Future reporting criterion	Data collected by State?	Included in Fast-Start Finance (FSF) reports?
Status (provided, committed, and/or pledged)	No[a]	No
Private financial flows leveraged by bilateral climate finance, to the extent possible	No[a]	No[b]
Total amount (funding level) that is climate specific	Yes	Yes
Funding source (official development assistance, other official flows, other)	Yes	No
Financial instrument (grant, concessional loan, etc.)	Yes	Yes
Type of support (mitigation, adaptation, cross-cutting)	Yes	No[c]
Sector (energy, transport, etc.)	Yes	Yes
Additional information (parties should report, as appropriate, on project details and the implementing agency)	Yes	Yes
Explanation of how funds are climate-specific	Yes	No
Whether financial resources are new and additional and how this was determined	Yes	No

Source: GAO analysis of State data and information from the United Nations Framework Convention for Climate Change (Framework Convention).

Notes: To make the comparison shown in the table, we analyzed the reports of the Conference of the Parties to the Framework Convention in Durban (2011) and Doha (2012) and State FSF reports.

[34]U.N. Doc. FCCC/CP/2011/9/Add.1, decision 2/CP.17, ¶ 13 and Annex I. In addition to the new biennial reports, developed countries will also submit the sixth national communication to the Framework Convention secretariat in January 2014. Developed countries report to the Framework Convention secretariat through national communications and biennial reports with information on the steps the countries are taking or plan to take to implement the Framework Convention. Also, at the meeting of the Conference of the Parties in Durban in 2011, developed countries decided that in years when national communications are submitted, developed countries should submit the biennial reports as an annex to the national communications or as a separate report.

GAO-13-829 Climate Change

[a]State officials said they collect some of this information but not as specified in the new reporting guidelines.

[b]In the 2012 FSF report, State provided an example of private funds leveraged by OPIC.

[c]The 2012 FSF report included aggregate-level but not project-level information.

We identified six biennial reporting criteria that State will be expected to report on for climate finance contributions in 2014 but did not report on in the FSF reports, including two for which State does not currently collect data as fully as required by the Framework Convention's new reporting criteria (see table 3). State officials said that they have not determined how they will implement these 2014 reporting requirements and guidelines.

State does not currently collect all of the data needed to meet the following two criteria.

- *The annual status of climate finance contributions provided, committed, and/or pledged.* Beginning in 2014, developed countries will be required to report on the amount of their climate finance contributions provided, committed, and/or pledged and should explain the methodologies used to specify the funds in each category. State officials said that there are no agreed-upon definitions for provided, committed, and pledged in the Framework Convention and that countries may choose which status to use in filling out the table showing the status of their climate finance contributions. State has not defined these terms yet and does not collect status data on FSF funds according to these categories. State has some status information for FSF activities, but according to State officials, has not been collecting this information according to the terms in the Framework Convention reporting guidelines, as they are new guidelines.

- *Private financial flows leveraged by bilateral climate finance.* In 2011, the Conference of the Parties met in Durban and decided that developed countries should report in their biennial reports, to the extent possible, on private financial flows leveraged by bilateral climate finance and policies and measures that promote the scaling up of private investment in mitigation and adaptation activities in developing countries. In April 2013, State and Treasury convened a meeting to discuss how international donors could better coordinate to use public finance to mobilize private investment in climate-friendly infrastructure. However, State officials said that the parties did not focus on how they would incorporate private sector sources into future reporting on climate finance and that they will continue to work with the international community to develop a methodology for collecting the information. Adding information on private sources of financing will add a layer of complexity to the already difficult task of reporting on public sources of climate finance because, among other things, information related to the financing and implementing of private-sector projects is often proprietary.

State collects data for the following four elements, but did not include this information in the FSF reports.

- *The funding source (official development assistance, other official flows, or other)*. State did not provide this information in the FSF reports. According to State officials, State does collect this information for all agencies.

- *Type of support (mitigation, adaptation, cross-cutting)*. In 2014, developed countries will be required to report on the type of support provided—mitigation, adaptation, or cross-cutting (those activities that support both mitigation and adaptation), and to the extent possible, at the country, region, project, or program level. In the fiscal year 2012 FSF report, State provided only aggregated information on adaptation and mitigation contributions.

- *An explanation of how each country determined that its funds are climate-specific*. State had criteria it used to determine which activities counted as FSF for its internal reports and provided the criteria to agencies to help them determine which activities to include in their FSF submissions and which to exclude. Over the 2010 to 2012 FSF period, State refined the criteria to provide more guidance on what to count as an activity with a primary goal of addressing climate change versus what should count as having a climate-related benefit. In the 2012 FSF report, State provided some information on the methodology for counting activities with climate-related benefits and some examples of activities under each pillar. However, State did not publish the criteria in the FSF reports. State officials said that these definitions for future climate finance reporting are still being discussed with both the Framework Convention and the Development Assistance Committee of the Organisation for Economic Co-operation and Development (OECD). State officials also said that they expect to be guided, in part, by those discussions, but anticipate the criteria they use will be similar to those used for the FSF reports.

- *Whether financial resources are new and additional and how this was determined*. As mentioned earlier, the Framework Convention did not define "new and additional resources," and in developing the FSF reports State counted all funding for activities that address climate change in developing countries as "new and additional." However, State did not publicly define "new and additional" in its FSF reports, and will be required to do so in the 2014 biennial report.

To meet certain future reporting requirements and guidelines, developed countries will also need to provide information, such as total funding level and financial instrument, in two tables—one for contributions to multilateral funds and one for bilateral and regional contributions—for the previous 2 years.[35] The information on bilateral and regional contributions is to be reported for each recipient country, region, project, or program, to the extent possible. State officials said that they are still in the process of determining which is the most appropriate category—country, region, project, or program—to use for organizing the bilateral table. However, it is uncertain how State will meet the requirements to report on the data elements, such as status or financial instrument, if it reports at the country or region level since the myriad activities in a given country or region may involve a variety of financial instruments. State officials also said that they are still determining the best use of their existing FSF database for future required reporting, so it is currently unclear how State will collect and maintain the data needed for the 2014 report.

---

[35]In addition to the climate finance reporting requirements and guidelines for the Framework Convention parties, the United States also reports and will continue to report funding related to climate change through other venues, primarily the Credit Reporting System of the Development Assistance Committee at the OECD, and the Administration's Foreign Assistance Dashboard. A 2012 OMB bulletin provides guidance on reporting to the OECD and for the Foreign Assistance Dashboard website as part of the U.S. government's overall effort to make information on foreign assistance programs more transparent. The Foreign Assistance Dashboard is a key deliverable of the U.S. Government's Open Government Partnership National Action Plan to promote openness and transparency. The Dashboard serves as a tool to visualize foreign assistance data. It can be found at http://www.foreignassistance.gov. In addition, the OECD developed a marker system in collaboration with the Framework Convention aimed at tracking resource flows for climate change activities. The markers, known as Rio Markers, categorize aid activities to indicate whether or not an activity targets climate change mitigation or adaptation as a principal or significant objective. Reporting with Rio Markers became mandatory with the 2007 report to the OECD.

Determining Effectiveness of FSF Activities Poses Challenges; State and USAID Are Refining Their Approach to Monitoring and Evaluating Activities That Address Climate Change

The overall effectiveness of U.S. FSF activities is difficult to determine because of the challenges involved in monitoring and evaluating assistance to address climate change. Measuring the effects of individual activities within the larger context of global climate change is difficult, and many activities are just beginning to be implemented. State, USAID, and Treasury fund FSF activities included in the GCCI. As part of this initiative, State and USAID are refining performance indicators to improve monitoring of the results of their activities that address climate change. USAID is also drafting an evaluation plan for its GCCI activities, although no evaluations have been completed. Treasury does not directly monitor and evaluate its GCCI funding, but requires the multilateral institutions that receive and implement this funding to conduct monitoring and evaluation. Other agencies, including MCC, Ex-Im, and OPIC funded activities that were not part of GCCI, and these agencies take varying approaches to monitoring and evaluating these activities based on their respective missions and requirements.

Linking Climate Change Assistance to Outcomes Poses Challenges

Efforts to monitor the outcomes and evaluate the longer-term impact of assistance to address climate change involve several key challenges. Measuring the effect of U.S.-supported mitigation activities on climate change involves estimating what greenhouse gas emissions might have been if the assistance had not been provided. Likewise, measuring the effect of adaptation activities involves finding ways to estimate what climate damages might otherwise have occurred. In addition, because U.S. assistance to address climate change encompasses a wide range of activities, the appropriate type of monitoring and evaluation depends on each activity and its intent. Specific challenges to monitoring and evaluating this assistance include the following:

- *Assistance intended to address climate change occurs within a larger context.* In cases where U.S. funded activities are intended to decrease emissions, it is difficult to measure their effect on climate change when overall emissions and atmospheric carbon dioxide levels are increasing. Climate change results from the long-term accumulation of greenhouse gases in the atmosphere, and the Environmental Protection Agency projects that greenhouse gas concentrations will continue to increase in the future unless annual emissions decrease substantially. In addition, according to a 2009 U.S. Global Change Research Program assessment, the atmospheric concentrations of carbon dioxide—the primary greenhouse gas—have been building up in the Earth's atmosphere since the beginning of the industrial era in the mid-1700s, primarily due to the burning of fossil fuels and the clearing of forests.[36] As noted by the National Research Council in 2012, current carbon dioxide concentrations are nearly 40 percent higher than preindustrial levels, and, according to ice core data, higher than at any point in the past 800,000 years.[37]

- *Monitoring and evaluation of activities under the three GCCI pillars involves varying assumptions and uncertainties.* For example, for projects under the clean energy pillar, USAID and State monitor the reductions in greenhouse gas emissions attributable to U.S. assistance. However, attributing emissions reductions to a clean energy project requires an assumption that the project displaced existing or future sources of more carbon-intensive sources of electricity, such as that generated by burning fossil fuels. Therefore, the results and accuracy of monitoring and evaluation of these projects will depend on the validity of the underlying assumptions, which may be difficult to determine. It is also difficult to determine whether individual forest protection projects under the sustainable landscapes pillar materially influence overall emissions from forests if the projects do not address the social and economic forces contributing to forest degradation or destruction. Deforestation and the conversion of forested lands to agriculture in developing countries is a major source of greenhouse gas emissions. Efforts to protect or enhance forests can lead to the increased absorption of carbon dioxide from the atmosphere. However, our prior work has found that protecting a forest does not necessarily decrease the demand for the timber or conversion of forested land to other uses.[38] Instead, it may shift demand to other unprotected forested lands through a process

---

[36]Thomas R. Karl, Jerry M. Melillo, and Thomas C. Peterson, eds., *Global Climate Change Impacts in the United States* (New York, NY: Cambridge University Press, 2009). This document, referred to as the 2009 National Climate Assessment, is in the process of being updated, as the Global Change Research Act of 1990 requires that a scientific assessment be provided to the President and Congress not less frequently than every 4 years. See information on the 2013 National Climate Assessment at http://www.globalchange.gov/what-we-do/assessment.

[37]See National Research Council, *Climate Change: Evidence, Impacts, and Choices* (Washington, D.C.: 2012). The National Research Council is the operating arm of the National Academy of Sciences and National Academy of Engineering.

[38]GAO, *Climate Change Issues: Options for Addressing Challenges to Carbon Offset Quality*, GAO-11-345 (Washington, D.C.: Feb.15, 2011).

known as emissions "leakage."[39] In addition, our prior work has identified challenges in measuring carbon stored by forests due to scientific uncertainties and the potential for protected forests to later suffer degradation from fire, storms, insect infestation, or future changes in land management.[40]

- *Directly linking some activities to climate change outcomes is difficult.* USAID officials stated that some specific activities intended to address climate change, such as training and capacity building, are particularly difficult to link directly to climate change outcomes, such as reductions in greenhouse gas emissions. For example, some USAID projects focus on capacity building to support recipient countries' regulatory or legal reforms and national climate change plans, and may not have a direct link to greenhouse gas emissions. While these activities may provide important benefits in building local capacity, USAID officials acknowledged the challenges in linking these types of activities to emissions reductions. In Mexico, for example, USAID's assistance has focused, in part, on supporting planning and policy development, including supporting the implementation of the country's recently passed national climate change law. USAID officials stated that it was not clear how these types of activities will translate into greenhouse gas emissions reductions. However, State and USAID officials also emphasized that capacity-building efforts can yield important longer-term benefits, even if they are difficult to link to short-term outcomes.

- *Assistance to address climate change is relatively new, and it is too early to assess outcomes.* According to U.S. officials, many of the U.S. FSF activities have not been completed and, in some cases, are just beginning to be implemented. As discussed earlier, during our country site visits, we found examples of U.S. FSF projects counted toward the fiscal year 2010 or 2011 FSF totals that were only beginning implementation. For example, according to MCC officials, MCC's Green Prosperity project in Indonesia just began to be implemented after the Compact entered into force in April 2013. While

---

[39]USAID officials commented that they see U.S. support for countries' low emissions development strategies, which promote national-level greenhouse gas inventories and policy reforms, as a response to "leakage." These officials commented that by monitoring greenhouse gas emissions and forest cover nationwide, countries will be able to monitor the net effect of all sustainable forest and land use efforts.

[40]GAO-11-345.

MCC is developing a monitoring and evaluation plan for this project, it is too early to assess its results or impact. Also in Indonesia, USAID's Forest and Climate Support project has been slower to begin implementation than originally anticipated, according to project officials. Implementing officials said that no project evaluations have been completed, although a midterm evaluation was beginning during the time of our visit.

State and USAID Are Refining Indicators to Monitor Climate Change Activities, and USAID Is Developing an Evaluation Plan

State and USAID Are Refining Their Climate Change Indicators

State and USAID use a combination of standard and custom indicators to monitor U.S. FSF activities that are part of the GCCI and non-GCCI activities reported to have climate-related benefits. Following the launch of the GCCI in 2010, State and USAID developed a *GCCI Indicator Handbook* to provide guidance for project implementers in monitoring activities intended to address climate change, and the agencies have continued to revise these indicators to improve measurement of climate change activities. The handbook currently contains seven standard indicators to monitor the performance of State and USAID's assistance to address climate change, including, according to USAID officials, two required outcome indicators. The first outcome indicator measures the quantity of greenhouse gas emissions reduced or sequestered as a result of the U.S. clean energy and sustainable landscapes projects. The second outcome indicator measures the number of stakeholders with increased capacity to adapt to the impacts of climate change as a result of U.S. adaptation projects. The remaining five indicators track outputs,[41] such as the number of people receiving training and the number of days of technical assistance provided (see table 4).

---

[41]Outputs measure the direct products and services delivered by programs or projects; outcomes measure the results of those products and services.

Table 4: State and USAID's Standard Global Climate Change Indicators

	Indicator	Indicator type
1	Quantity of greenhouse gas emissions, measured in metric tons of carbon dioxide equivalent,[a] reduced or sequestered as a result of U.S. assistance	Outcome[b]
2[c]	Person hours of training completed in climate change supported by U.S. assistance	Output
	Number of people receiving training in Global Climate Change as a result of U.S. assistance	Output
3	Amount of investment leveraged in U.S. dollars, from private and public sources, for climate change as a result of U.S. assistance	Output
4	Number of institutions with improved capacity to address climate change issues as a result of U.S. assistance	Output
5	Number of stakeholders with increased capacity to adapt to the impacts of climate variability and change as a result of U.S. assistance	Outcome[d]
6	Number of days of U.S.-funded technical assistance addressing climate change that is provided to counterparts or stakeholders	Output
7	Number of laws, policies, strategies, plans, agreements, or regulations addressing climate change (mitigation or adaptation) and/or biodiversity conservation officially proposed, adopted, or implemented as a result of U.S. assistance	Output

Source: U.S. Agency for International Development (USAID).

Notes:

[a]The Environmental Protection Agency defines carbon dioxide equivalent as a metric measure used to compare greenhouse gases based upon their global warming potential.

[b]According to USAID officials, this indicator is required for clean energy and sustainable landscapes projects.

[c]Either version of this indicator can be used to report on training related to global climate change.

[d]According to USAID officials, this indicator is required for adaptation projects.

These standard indicators are linked to U.S. foreign assistance strategic objectives and intended to facilitate the aggregating and reporting of quantitative information common to U.S. assistance across recipient countries. State and USAID use the standard indicators in performance reports that summarize project activities, achievements, and difficulties encountered. USAID officials described the *GCCI Indicator Handbook* as a first-generation resource for missions and stated that they continue to seek opportunities to improve the agency's climate change indicators, including by researching indicators used by other agencies and donors.

In addition to standard indicators, State and USAID use custom indicators to capture dimensions of projects that are specific to individual countries and that are not reflected in the standard indicators. For example, in Indonesia USAID uses a custom indicator to track the number of people with access to modern energy services as a result of renewable energy technologies through U.S. assistance. At the project level, USAID's Indonesia Marine and Climate Support project includes custom indicators on the number of people reached through climate change public awareness campaigns and the number of risk and vulnerability assessments completed by local governments.

USAID Is Developing an Evaluation Plan for Climate Change Activities

USAID has begun drafting an overall evaluation plan for the GCCI in accordance with its recently issued evaluation policy, and expects to complete this initial evaluation plan in 2013. While USAID has not yet completed evaluations of programs or activities under the initiative, it has begun some evaluations, including evaluations of pilot programs intended to integrate climate change goals into other USAID programs in selected countries. In January 2011, USAID issued a new policy that defines agency requirements for evaluations, including the commitment that 3 percent of program budgets, on average, must be devoted to external evaluations. The new policy defines two types of evaluations:

- *Performance evaluations* focus on what projects have achieved, how they are being implemented, what expected results are occurring, and other questions related to program design, management, and operational decision making.

- *Impact evaluations* measure the change in development outcomes attributable to a defined intervention and require a rigorous counterfactual to control for factors other than the intervention that might account for the observed change.

USAID's policy requires all large projects[42] to have at least one performance evaluation and that evaluations be timed so that findings will be available to inform decisions about new strategies, project designs, and procurements. The policy further requires activities to undergo impact evaluation, if feasible, if they use new approaches or untested hypotheses and if USAID anticipates expanding them.[43] As previously

---

[42]USAID defines large projects as those whose dollar value equals or exceeds the average project value for the operating unit.

[43]Consistent with USAID's evaluation policy, State issued its own evaluation policy in February 2012, which also includes a requirement that large programs be evaluated at least once.

discussed, USAID issued its Climate Change and Development Strategy in 2012, and USAID officials commented that the evaluation policy has since shaped the agency's approach to how it will evaluate its assistance intended to address climate change by putting greater emphasis on long-term impact evaluations. USAID's climate change strategy includes a results framework with strategic objectives and intermediate results, including a combined strategic objective for clean energy and sustainable landscapes, and a separate strategic objective for adaptation.

USAID officials stated that the development of the evaluation plan included revising and updating the results frameworks to provide separate and more detailed frameworks for each of the three GCCI pillars: adaptation, clean energy, and sustainable landscapes. According to USAID officials, these results frameworks will provide a more detailed hypothesis, or a theory of change, to underpin USAID's work in the three pillars. These officials further stated that in developing these results frameworks, they have reached out to monitoring and evaluation consultants and are conducting literature reviews to assess the hypotheses and assumptions outlined in the frameworks, including, for example, their assertion that a country's enabling environment is key to reducing greenhouse gas emissions. In addition, these officials said that they are conducting a manual inventory of programs addressing climate change across USAID missions worldwide and selecting missions to conduct impact evaluations of these programs.

Although the evaluation plan has not been completed, USAID officials stated that the agency has initiated some evaluations of its pilot program to integrate climate change goals into other programs, such as the Feed the Future initiative. So far, USAID has competitively selected 10 USAID overseas missions for pilot integration projects, including a project in Ethiopia that aims to improve resilience to climate change by helping communities address conflicts over scarce natural resources. USAID officials stated that several of the missions participating in this pilot have developed evaluation plans.

Treasury Delegates Monitoring and Evaluation of FSF Activities to Multilateral Institutions

In contrast to USAID's and State's bilateral programs, Treasury officials stated that they require the monitoring and evaluation of multilateral FSF activities funded through the Climate Investment Funds (CIF) and the Global Environment Facility (GEF) to be conducted by the multilateral development banks and other international institutions that implement these activities. These implementing institutions have their own monitoring and evaluation processes, including requirements both at the trust fund level (e.g., the Clean Technology Fund) and the implementing agency level (e.g., the World Bank). Treasury officials stated that the department does not directly fund CIF or GEF projects in specific countries, but provides annual contributions to these trust funds, which are implemented by multilateral development banks and international institutions, such as the Asian Development Bank or the United Nations Development Programme. Treasury officials stated that they lack the resources to directly monitor or evaluate CIF or GEF projects, and instead rely on a common system of oversight of these funds through participation on their governing boards. The Treasury officials stated that as members of the CIF and GEF boards, they review regular progress reporting on country programs and individual projects. GEF officials told us, for example, that Treasury actively participates on the GEF Council reviewing project reporting and querying implementers on project results. GEF officials further stated that implementing organizations, such as the World Bank, conduct performance monitoring using standard GEF indicators and tracking tools and also conduct final project evaluations.[44]

Each of the CIF funds has a results framework that is applied to individual country programs and, according to Treasury officials, serves as the basis for future monitoring and evaluation of the impact, outcomes, and outputs of the CIF-supported activities. The responsibility for reporting on progress rests with the CIF's country focal points and with multilateral development bank staff. For example, the multilateral development banks implementing Clean Technology Fund projects in a country are required to report annually on the progress on core indicators. More specifically, the fund's Geothermal Clean Energy Investment Project in Indonesia, financed and implemented through the World Bank, includes results indicators on annual greenhouse gas emissions reductions and increased supply of geothermal capacity.

In addition, each of the multilateral development banks has its own monitoring and evaluation process, and the banks' evaluation units conduct evaluations of CIF projects as part of their regular responsibilities. Treasury officials stated that a broader evaluation of the CIF is being conducted by an independent committee and representatives

---

[44]According to Treasury officials, for the bilateral Tropical Forest Conservation Act (TFCA) activities that Treasury funds, Treasury also conducts oversight through (1) participation in the interagency group that monitors TFCA issues, (2) reports from local TFCA programs, and (3) evaluations of individual country programs that Treasury funds through allocations to USAID. The U.S. government, according to these Treasury officials, also has direct oversight of local programs through its participation on local TFCA country boards.

of multilateral development bank evaluation units, and is due to be completed in 2013.

Other Agencies' Approaches to Monitoring and Evaluating FSF Activities Vary

The other key agencies that contributed to FSF—MCC, Ex-Im, and OPIC—funded activities that were not part of the GCCI, and these agencies' approaches to monitoring and evaluation vary based on their respective missions and requirements. These agencies' funding supports activities with reported climate-related benefits.

- *MCC monitoring and evaluation focuses primarily on poverty reduction.* MCC's mission is to reduce poverty through economic growth, and MCC officials stated that it monitors and evaluates projects primarily for progress in achieving this goal using economic indicators. According to MCC officials, MCC supports low carbon economic development and helps partner countries address the risks of climate change when it is consistent with MCC's core mission and supports the primary and development objectives of a compact's primary poverty alleviation goal. For example, MCC's monitoring and evaluation plan for the Green Prosperity Project in Indonesia is focused on indicators related to increasing productivity and incomes, but the plan also includes indicators related to expanding renewable energy capacity and improving sustainable land use and forest management.

- *Ex-Im monitors its projects counted as FSF according to broader agency requirements.* Ex-Im's primary mission is to assist in financing the export of U.S. goods and services to international markets. According to Ex-Im officials, Ex-Im does not have climate change indicators or related monitoring and evaluation requirements for its projects, but it monitors its projects counted as FSF according to broader agency requirements, including monitoring to ensure repayment. The officials also told us that for projects that Ex-Im determines may produce greenhouse gas emissions in excess of 25,000 metric tons of carbon dioxide equivalent per year, the bank requires applicants to provide information on the anticipated quantity of greenhouse gas emissions.

- *OPIC monitors greenhouse gas emissions of its projects to track progress against a mandated emission goal.* OPIC is the U.S. government's development finance institution and its primary mission is to mobilize private capital to promote development and advance U.S. foreign policy. OPIC has a congressional requirement to achieve a 30-percent reduction in the greenhouse gas emissions of its portfolio over a 10-year period,[45] and it monitors and reports annually on the greenhouse gas emissions associated with its financing to track progress toward achieving this goal. OPIC also reports on the anticipated renewable energy megawatts generated and greenhouse gas emissions avoided for selected clean energy projects, including the projects counted as FSF.

Conclusions

Assistance to developing countries to address the causes and effects of climate change has become increasingly important for the United States. Diplomatically, this assistance shows the United States' commitment to its broader international agreements to address climate change. It also demonstrates the United States' commitments to assist developing nations that face the most significant adverse impacts of climate change. As a member of the Conference of the Parties in Durban in 2011, the United States agreed to additional reporting requirements and guidelines beginning in 2014 but has not determined how to fulfill this agreement. State made progress in its ability to collect and report on assistance aimed to address climate change to developing countries and voluntarily submitted three FSF reports containing information on the range of U.S. FSF activities. However, challenges remain, including determining a method for incorporating private sector finance into U.S. climate finance totals. According to State officials, the FSF reports helped meet U.S. diplomatic objectives by informing recipient countries of the range of U.S. climate finance activities occurring in these countries. However, if State does not meet future reporting requirements, it will be more difficult to demonstrate to international parties the United States' commitment to climate finance. While State has started working with its international counterparts to address some of the future reporting requirements, our findings show that State does not currently collect the data necessary to fully meet the 2014 Framework Convention reporting requirements and guidelines.

State's challenges in collecting and reporting on foreign assistance intended to address climate change are compounded by the lack of a dedicated budget code to track over $1 billion in USAID climate change assistance, due to the placement of climate change as a sub-element within State and USAID's foreign assistance standardized program

---

[45]OPIC's requirement is to reduce the greenhouse gas emissions associated with projects and sub-projects in its portfolio by 30 percent over a 10-year period from June 30, 2008, and by 50 percent over a 15-year period from June 30, 2008. 22 U.S.C. § 2191b.

structure. Without a specific line item for climate assistance for developing countries, the agency must manually review data for over a hundred missions. Without better accounting for this assistance at USAID, both agencies will likely spend substantial and potentially unnecessary resources manually tracking U.S. funding. Improving this accounting may involve tradeoffs that merit consideration before revising the standardized program structure. For example, changes to the placement of climate change within the program structure may affect the accounting for other types of environmental assistance. On the other hand, the United States has made international commitments to collect and report on climate change assistance to developing countries as part of the administration's efforts to enhance the transparency of foreign assistance. Furthermore, providing this information could assist Congress in its oversight of foreign assistance for climate change activities.

Recommendations for Executive Action

We recommend that the Secretary of State take the following two actions:

1. To ensure the United States meets its future reporting requirements and guidelines under the Framework Convention, we recommend that State determine how it will collect and report climate finance information that will be required beginning in 2014. In doing so, State should review the capabilities of its current data collection and reporting process and consider what changes, if any, are needed to meet the requirements and guidelines.

2. As State conducts reviews of the foreign assistance standardized program structure, we recommend that State, in consultation with USAID, consider the merits of elevating climate change within the program structure to provide.a specific budget code that improves tracking of USAID climate change assistance.

Agency Comments

We provided a draft of this report for comment to State, USAID, Treasury, MCC, Ex-Im, and OPIC. We received written comments from State, which are reproduced in full in appendix II. State agreed with our recommendations and expressed willingness to take action. We also received technical comments from State, USAID, Treasury, and MCC, which we incorporated throughout our report as appropriate.

We are sending copies of this report to appropriate congressional committees; the Secretaries of State and the Treasury, the Administrator of USAID, the Chairman of the Export-Import Bank, and the Chief Executive Officers of the Millennium Challenge Corporation and the

Overseas Private Investment Corporation. This report will also be available at no charge on GAO's Web site at http://www.gao.gov.

If you or your staff have any questions about this report, please contact Thomas Melito at (202) 512-9601 or melitot@gao.gov, or J. Alfredo Gomez at (202) 512-4101 or gomezj@gao.gov. Contact points for our Offices of Congressional Relations and Public Affairs may be found on the last page of this report. GAO staff who made key contributions to this report are listed in appendix III.

Sincerely yours,

Thomas Melito
Director, International Affairs and Trade

J. Alfredo Gomez
Director, Natural Resources and Environment

Appendix I: Objectives, Scope, and Methodology

This report examines (1) the extent to which the United States contributed to fast-start finance (FSF) and the types of activities this funding supported, (2) how the Department of State (State) collected and reported data on U.S. FSF funding and its plans for future reporting, and (3) what is known about the effectiveness of U.S. FSF activities. To address these objectives, we focused primarily on the six agencies that provided over 95 percent of U.S. FSF assistance in fiscal years 2010 through 2012: State, the U.S. Agency for International Development (USAID), the Department of the Treasury (Treasury), the Millennium Challenge Corporation (MCC), the Export-Import Bank of the United States (Ex-Im), and the Overseas Private Investment Corporation (OPIC). We reviewed and analyzed documents and interviewed agency officials from these six agencies and from the U.S. Trade and Development Agency (USTDA), the Environmental Protection Agency (EPA), and the U.S. Forest Service, as well as officials from the United Nations Framework Convention on Climate Change (Framework Convention), the Organisation for Economic Co-operation and Development, and nongovernmental organizations. We conducted fieldwork in three countries—Ethiopia, Indonesia, and Mexico—that we selected on the basis of FSF funding levels and sources; areas of focus (adaptation, clean energy, and sustainable landscapes); project implementation status; geographic diversity; country income level; recommendations from agencies; and congressional interest. In these countries, we met with U.S. embassy officials and implementing partners, host-country government officials, multilateral development banks, and other bilateral donors. We also visited project sites and met with local implementing partners and recipients of the assistance.

To understand the extent to which the United States contributed to FSF and the types of activities this funding supported, we reviewed Framework Convention climate finance agreements and requirements, as well as government-wide and agency specific initiatives and strategies, and planning and programming documents. We reviewed FSF activity and funding data submitted by these agencies to State, and reviewed State's consolidated FSF data. We also reviewed State's and other countries' FSF reports and submissions to the Framework Convention. To assess the reliability of State's FSF data, we interviewed agency officials about data quality control procedures and reviewed relevant documentation. In addition, agency officials walked us through their database and discussed the various controls used. We determined that the data were sufficiently reliable for the purposes of this report.

To examine how State collected and reported data on U.S. FSF funding, we reviewed and analyzed FSF funding data submitted by the agencies to State and reviewed State's own data on FSF. In addition, we reviewed State's database for maintaining FSF submissions for the fiscal year 2012 FSF report and interviewed State officials responsible for compiling the data and creating the FSF reports. We determined that the data were sufficiently reliable for our purposes. In addition, we reviewed the criteria used by State to determine the FSF eligibility of activities listed in agency submissions. We also compared the guidance for agencies on FSF submissions from State and the Office of Management and Budget (OMB). To examine State's plans for future reporting, we reviewed State reports and the reports of the Framework Convention Conference of the Parties meetings. We interviewed agency officials from the six agencies listed above, as well as officials from EPA, U.S. Forest Service, USTDA, and OMB. In addition, we obtained disbursement status data from the USAID program offices in Ethiopia and Indonesia for all FSF activities for fiscal years 2010 through 2012. USAID in Mexico was unable to provide us with disbursement status data for their FSF activities.

To examine what is known about the effectiveness of U.S. FSF activities, we focused on the six agencies listed above. To examine how these agencies monitored and evaluated the effectiveness of their FSF activities, we reviewed agency goals and indicators, monitoring and evaluation plans and reports, and interviewed agency officials.

We conducted this performance audit from May 2012 to September 2013 in accordance with generally accepted government auditing standards. Those standards require that we plan and perform the audit to obtain sufficient, appropriate evidence to provide a reasonable basis for our findings and conclusions based on our audit objectives. We believe that the evidence obtained provides a reasonable basis for our findings and conclusions based on our audit objectives.

Appendix II: Comments from the Department of State

United States Department of State

Washington, D.C. 20520

Dr. Loren Yager
Managing Director
International Affairs and Trade
Government Accountability Office
441 G Street, N.W.
Washington, D.C. 20548-0001

SEP 0 9 2013

Dear Dr. Yager:

We appreciate the opportunity to review your draft report, "CLIMATE CHANGE: State Should Further Improve Its Reporting on Financial Support to Developing Countries to Meet Future Requirements" GAO Job Code 320914.

The enclosed Department of State comments are provided for incorporation with this letter as an appendix to the final report.

If you have any questions concerning this response, please contact Teresa Hobgood, Senior Policy Advisor, Bureau of Oceans and International Environmental and Scientific Affairs at (202) 647-3550.

Sincerely,

James L. Millette

cc: GAO – J. Alfredo Gomez
     OES – Dr. Kerri-Ann Jones
     State/OIG – Norm Brown

Department of State Comments on GAO Draft Report

CLIMATE CHANGE: State Should Further Improve Its Reporting on Financial Support to Developing Countries to Meet Future Requirements
(GAO-13-829, GAO Code 320914)

Thank you for the opportunity to comment on the draft report on reporting on financial data for international climate change assistance to developing countries. The Department of State appreciates GAO's analysis and recommendations.

Climate change is one of this century's signal global challenges. It works against virtually every U.S. foreign policy goal – economic development, peace and stability, and poverty alleviation. The United States is leading the effort to forge a new global agreement that would apply to all countries. We are using diplomatic tools and development dollars to prepare vulnerable nations for climate impacts and reduce the likelihood of dangerous climate change.

Climate change is already a top foreign policy priority for many nations, and it will only grow in prominence in coming years. It threatens to disrupt agriculture, fisheries, and water supply for many regions of the world, and if left unchecked, will threaten the continued viability of low-lying nations in the Pacific and Asia, including strong U.S. allies. As recent damage from storms such as Sandy and droughts in the nation's heartland suggest, projected increases in the frequency and intensity of extreme weather events also have the potential to devastate communities and impose enormous costs in the United States in coming decades.

Addressing climate change successfully will require prompt and decisive action by all nations. The United States, as the world's preeminent economic and technological power and one of the largest emitters of greenhouse gases, must lead. The Administration has made it a priority to develop a sensible global response to the challenge. Through successive rounds of negotiations, we have helped move the world from an emissions regime that only includes a small subset of countries and emissions to an approach in which all major economies, including the world's emerging economies, have committed to take specific, meaningful and transparent actions and meet specific targets by 2020.

This represents significant progress, but there is much more to do. This generation has a responsibility to leave a cleaner, safer and more stable world to all those who come after us, and the world is not on track to reduce emissions to levels that will enable us to avoid dangerous climate impacts. As a result, the Administration will

2

continue to work as a matter of priority to develop a global effort that applies to all that can enable us to meet this challenge successfully.

Our foreign assistance funding enables us to play a leading role in this global effort. Through our foreign assistance, we are able to lead efforts to promote cleaner and more efficient energy, conserve the world's remaining tropical rainforests, phase down chemicals with high global warming potential, and support the poorest and most vulnerable countries and communities in their efforts to cope with the adverse impacts of severe weather events and climate change. Our investments are consistent with and support the Administration's broader development agenda. Our ability to meet major international funding commitments thus far has helped secure the agreement of developing countries to take on specific commitments to reduce greenhouse gas emissions and to report and be reviewed on their progress.

The Administration has devoted much attention to investing and prioritizing strategically. In order to maximize our assistance funding, we have taken significant steps to integrate climate change considerations into all relevant development assistance activities. We are working to leverage private investment, including foreign direct investment and we are supporting developing countries' efforts to determine the most effective approaches to address climate change, so that they can make a robust contribution to the global effort over time.

We are also actively engaging the major emerging economies, whose emissions are projected to grow over coming decades, and whose cooperation and engagement in this issue, along with our own, is essential to leaving a positive legacy for future generations.

The Department of State appreciates the GAO's recognition of the improvements made in collecting and reporting on our fulfillment of the "Fast Start" climate finance commitment. Regarding GAO Recommendation #1, the Department is actively preparing to provide public reports through the UN Framework Convention on Climate Change (UNFCCC) that will provide meaningful information following the extensive information that the United States provided through the three Fast Start Finance reports that were the focus of this GAO study. Although some decisions remain regarding the precise nature of future U.S. reporting, the Department is prepared to comply with the new UNFCCC reporting guidelines. In line with GAO's recommendation, the Department will continue to review the capabilities of its data collection and reporting process and consider what changes, if any, are needed.

3

Regarding GAO Recommendation #2, the State Department and USAID are in the
process of reviewing the foreign assistance Standardized Program Structure and
Definitions (SPSD). Proposed changes would further improve tracking of
international climate change assistance and enhance the transparency of reporting
on climate change expenditures for activities with a primary goal of addressing
climate change. Three new Program Areas that address the three pillars of the
Global Climate Change Initiative (GCCI) have been proposed for the updated
SPSD: Climate Change – Adaptation, Climate Change – Clean Energy, and
Climate Change – Sustainable Landscapes. New "Elements" proposed under each
Program Area would enable increased specificity in our budget planning. Creating
these new SPSD Areas and Elements would enable the State Department and
USAID to raise the three pillars of the GCCI in the State-USAID budget code
hierarchy to better collect GCCI-specific information and emphasize the
increasingly central role that climate change plays in the United States'
international development and diplomacy strategy. Pending Department approval
and availability of funds for new database systems, utilization of the updated SPSD
is expected to begin with the FY 2016 budget formulation.

The Department of State appreciates the review of reporting on U.S. climate
change assistance to developing countries that the GAO has undertaken.

Appendix III: GAO Contacts and Staff Acknowledgments

GAO Contacts	Thomas Melito, Director, International Affairs and Trade, (202) 512-9601, or melitot@gao.gov.
	J. Alfredo Gomez, Director, Natural Resources and Environment, (202) 512-4101, gomezj@gao.gov.
Staff Acknowledgments	In addition to the contacts named above, Christine Broderick (Assistant Director), Michael Hix (Assistant Director), Sada Aksartova, Ming Chen, Debbie Chung, Marissa Dondoe, Cindy Gilbert, Jeremy Latimer, Grace Lui, and Alana Miller made key contributions to this report.

GAO's Mission	The Government Accountability Office, the audit, evaluation, and investigative arm of Congress, exists to support Congress in meeting its constitutional responsibilities and to help improve the performance and accountability of the federal government for the American people. GAO examines the use of public funds; evaluates federal programs and policies; and provides analyses, recommendations, and other assistance to help Congress make informed oversight, policy, and funding decisions. GAO's commitment to good government is reflected in its core values of accountability, integrity, and reliability.
Obtaining Copies of GAO Reports and Testimony	The fastest and easiest way to obtain copies of GAO documents at no cost is through GAO's website (http://www.gao.gov). Each weekday afternoon, GAO posts on its website newly released reports, testimony, and correspondence. To have GAO e-mail you a list of newly posted products, go to http://www.gao.gov and select "E-mail Updates."
Order by Phone	The price of each GAO publication reflects GAO's actual cost of production and distribution and depends on the number of pages in the publication and whether the publication is printed in color or black and white. Pricing and ordering information is posted on GAO's website, http://www.gao.gov/ordering.htm. Place orders by calling (202) 512-6000, toll free (866) 801-7077, or TDD (202) 512-2537. Orders may be paid for using American Express, Discover Card, MasterCard, Visa, check, or money order. Call for additional information.
Connect with GAO	Connect with GAO on Facebook, Flickr, Twitter, and YouTube. Subscribe to our RSS Feeds or E-mail Updates. Listen to our Podcasts. Visit GAO on the web at www.gao.gov.
To Report Fraud, Waste, and Abuse in Federal Programs	Contact: Website: http://www.gao.gov/fraudnet/fraudnet.htm E-mail: fraudnet@gao.gov Automated answering system: (800) 424-5454 or (202) 512-7470
Congressional Relations	Katherine Siggerud, Managing Director, siggerudk@gao.gov, (202) 512-4400, U.S. Government Accountability Office, 441 G Street NW, Room 7125, Washington, DC 20548
Public Affairs	Chuck Young, Managing Director, youngc1@gao.gov, (202) 512-4800 U.S. Government Accountability Office, 441 G Street NW, Room 7149 Washington, DC 20548

Please Print on Recycled Paper.